# Our Garden

by Jessica Quilty

illustrated by Nicole Wong

PEARSON

Scott
Foresman

Editorial Offices: Glenview, Illinois • Parsippany, New Jersey • New York, New York
Sales Offices: Needham, Massachusetts • Duluth, Georgia • Glenview, Illinois
Coppell, Texas • Ontario, California • Mesa, Arizona

Every day on the way to school we walked
by an empty lot. The grass was overgrown and
littered with things people had thrown away.
There were pieces of wood, empty bottles and
cans, and old tires all over the ground. Years ago
there had been a store there, but the store had
closed and the building was torn down. Since
then, no one had cared for the empty lot.

"All that litter makes our city look dirty," Kate said one day. "We could clean out that lot and make it a nice place for people to enjoy."

"We could turn it into a park!" said Jim.

"Or a basketball court!" said John.

Then I had an idea. "I know what we can do," I said. "We can plant a beautiful garden. That would give this old lot new life!"

"A garden?" asked my friends. "That's a great idea!" they agreed.

We told our parents all about our idea. They were excited about our plan and wanted to help. They suggested that we go to City Hall and talk with the mayor of our city. He would know if we would be allowed to plant our garden on the empty lot.

The next day after school we all met with the mayor to discuss our plan. "That's a wonderful idea!" exclaimed Mayor Smith. "Children, you may begin work on your garden as soon as you'd like!" he told us excitedly.

Soon, summer vacation began. The weather
was sunny and warm. We had plenty of free
time, but we would not be lazy that summer. We
were ready to begin our work at the old lot.

On the first day, we looked all around the
lot to decide what needed to be done. "What a
mess!" everybody said.

"Don't worry. We can clean this up," I said.
It was a big job, but we were ready to work
together as partners to clean up the lot.

Jim picked up trash. Kate collected all the newspaper for recycling. We worked hard and did not cheat in our effort.

Our parents had their regular jobs to go to during the day. They didn't have much time to help us. But whenever they could they came by to pick up the sharp glass from broken bottles.

When Mayor Smith wasn't busy running the city, he came to help pull up weeds. "This old lot is looking great!" he exclaimed happily.

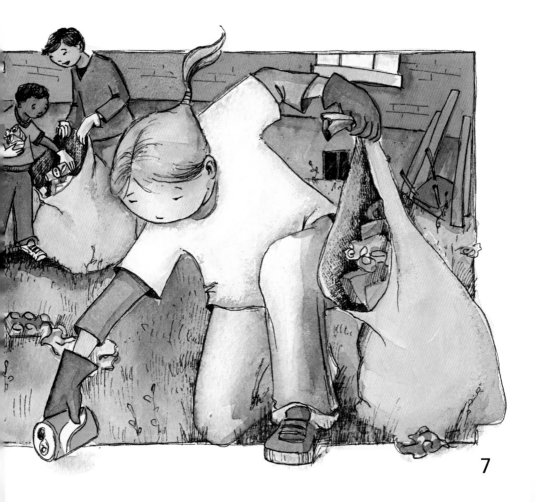

Soon it was time to decide what we would plant in our garden. We all had good ideas.

"Let's plant crops of tomatoes and potatoes to eat," said Kate.

"I'd like to have blue and yellow and red and orange flowers," said Jim.

"It would be fun to have a big tree for climbing and reading in the shade," I said. "And we could build a treehouse after our tree grows!"

"If we plan carefully," said John, "we can make our garden exactly how we'd like it to be!"

Later that day Mayor Smith and two other men arrived in a big truck. The truck was full of seeds and plants and soil for the garden.

"You are doing a wonderful thing for the people of our community," said the mayor. "The workers at City Hall have collected money to pay for the things you will need for the garden. It is a gift to you from our city!" he beamed.

We all cheered and thanked the mayor for his help.

We worked in our garden almost every day of that summer vacation. We spread healthy soil across the lot to coat the ground. Then we carefully planted our flower seeds. Tiny tomato vines went in one corner. Our parents helped us plant a young tree right in the middle of the garden. Then we placed bricks around the bottom of the tree.

The hot sun made us sweat. We didn't mind though. We knew that the sunlight would help our plants and flowers grow.

Each day, as we planted more of our garden, the empty lot became prettier.

One day, Mayor Smith brought a newspaper reporter to the lot. She was going to write a story about our garden for the city newspaper.

"These clever kids are bringing a wealth of community spirit to our city!" the mayor told her. "And you can quote me on that!"

The reporter talked with us and took our picture. We all held our shovels and smiled.

The people of our city read about our garden and came to see it for themselves. "Amazing!" they said, as they admired the tomato vines.

"Wonderful!" they exclaimed, as they walked around the tree.

Some people came to help. Mr. Yan brought a special plant for the garden. "It will bloom every year," he said.

Mr. and Mrs. Brown were experts at spotting weeds among the new plants.

At the end of the summer our garden was finished. Everyone was thrilled with the change.

Mayor Smith came to dedicate the garden to the children of our city. "We all have a beautiful new garden to enjoy thanks to these great kids!" he announced. "Let's all do our part to give it the care it will need."

Suddenly, it began to rain. We all got soaked. But we smiled and laughed, knowing that the rain was great for our thirsty new garden!

It rained for the next three days. Then on the fourth day we walked to the garden to see how things were growing. All our plants were in full bloom. The garden was more beautiful than ever.

Kate pointed to the tiny green tomatoes on the vines. "The tomatoes are growing so well!" she said proudly.

Jim collected beautiful flowers of every color for a bouquet.

Just before school started again, Kate said, "Let's pick our tomatoes before we get busy at school. They are red and ripe and ready to eat."

We invited Mayor Smith to help. The reporter who had followed the story of our garden was there too.

When we had finished our work, Mayor Smith took a big bite from a juicy red tomato. "Delicious!" he said with a smile. "Thank you!"

"Hooray for community spirit!" we cheered.

# Kids Help Out!

There are many ways you can help out your community and your neighbors. Turning an old lot into a garden may be just the beginning!

The Youth Volunteer Corps is an organization with branches all over the United States. In the Youth Volunteer Corps, kids help out every day by spending time with elderly or disabled people, tutoring other children, cleaning up parks and beaches, serving meals to the needy, and much more. Find out what you can do today to help out in your community!